Angels and Archangels in Reiki Practice

A practical guide

Haripriya Suraj

Copyright

© 2015, Acorn Gecko SRL

ALL RIGHTS RESERVED. This book contains material protected under International and Federal Copyright Laws and Treaties. Any unauthorized reprint or use of this material is prohibited. No part of this book may be reproduced or transmitted in any form or by any means, electronic or mechanical, including photocopying, recording, or by any information storage and retrieval system without express written permission from the publisher.

Reiki is not a replacement for medical assistance. Always seek professional medical support if you experience anything that requires it. Seek the services of a competent professional if expert assistance is required.

To fully understand and to be able to apply the techniques described in this book, the reader should already be introduced to the healing magic of Reiki.

Table of Contents

- Angels in Reiki Practice and Life 5
- Ten Signs from the Angels 11
- Setting and Fulfilling Intentions with Reiki and Archangel Michael 15
- Healing Fear with Reiki and Archangel Michael 19
- Cord Cutting with Reiki and Archangel Michael 23
- Build Your Healing Practice with Archangel Michael .. 27
- Safety and Protection with Archangel Michael 31
- Reiki Psychic Surgery with Archangel Raphael 35
- Reiki and Archangel Haniel 41
- Live Your Passions and Create a Colourful Life with Reiki and Archangel Haniel 45
- Communication with Departed Loved Ones: Reiki and Archangel Azrael 51
- Chakra Clearing with Reiki and Archangel Metatron .. 55
- Spiritual Power with Reiki, Raziel and Rainbow Energy 59
- Energy Clearing with Reiki and Archangel Jophiel 63
- The Power of the Violet Flame in Reiki Healing 67
- Guide to Archangels and Crystals 71
- Full Moon Healing with the Archangels 75
- Reiki Babies and Archangels – Part 1 79
- Reiki Babies and Archangels – Part 2 83
- Reiki Babies and Archangels – Part 3 87
- Stress Relief with the Angels 93
- Healing the Scars of Verbal Abuse with Reiki and the Angels 97
- Reiki with your Guides and Angels 101
- Five Ways to Heal Yourself in Sleep 105
- Connecting with our Guardian Angels 109
- Angel Communication through Letters 113
- Reiki Journal for Healing and Communication with Higher Realms 117
- Being a Reiki Angel on Earth 121
- Reiki and Spiritual Growth: A Personal Story 125
- About the Author 131

Angels in Reiki Practice and Life

The angels are among my best friends! The love I share with them is pure, sweet, unconditional and comforting.

My connection with the angels began a decade back, when they helped me cope with the passing on of my grandmother and helped remove a lot of fear and dark energy from my environment.

Thereafter, I have communicated with the angels at crucial moments in my life and expressed my deepest feelings to them. Whenever I could not share my feelings with human beings, I called upon these celestial beings and poured my heart out to them. And the best part is they always listened. Not only did they listen, but they also responded with unconditional love by sending help in the form of people or altered circumstances.

My connection with them deepened around the time that I decided to start teaching Reiki.

I was walking through a bookstore when my eyes happened to fall on the book *"Healing with the Angels" by Doreen Virtue*. I was instantly attracted to this book. Though a part of me really wanted that book, another part of me told me to wait for some time before reading it. So, I decided to wait.

A couple of months after I received the Master Degree attunement, I was guided to a workshop on *"Healing with the Angels"*. I also went on to read the book *"Healing with the Angels"* that I had seen at the bookstore. This was a period in life when I struggled to establish a Reiki Practice in circumstances that pushed me past my comfort zone. Doing the workshop and learning more about the angels was a significant milestone in my life. After doing this workshop, my connection with the angels deepened even further. They helped me set up my Reiki Practice. They also helped me face all the challenges that came along with choosing this path. They paved the way by helping me release and heal several patterns that were no longer serving me so I could be a better teacher myself.

As I went about establishing my Reiki practice, my connection with the angels became so strong that they are a part of everything I do today, including Reiki. I share all my ideas and feelings with them and they help me by working quietly behind the scenes.

Listed below are some aspects of my life, of which the angels form an integral part. If something resonates with you, know that the angels are trying to reach you through this piece of writing and wish to connect with you.

The Angels in Reiki Healing

The angels add a divine touch to Reiki healings and if you like the idea, you can try it yourself to see how it feels.

the assistance of the angels when I
for others or for my own self. When
for someone, I do an Angel Card
healing session and request those
ble to assist the client to step forward
place the angel cards in the healing
angels to help the client heal in the
ing an angel card reading also helps
ot cause of a client's issue and thereby
ce along with the Reiki healing.

The Angels in Reiki Attunements

The angels are present wherever healing work happens. So, it is only natural for them to be present during every Reiki attunement happening in the world!

During a Reiki attunement, I also request all those angels who would be of maximum help to the person receiving the attunement to step forward. I then go on to pick angel cards intuitively. I place all the angel cards in the attunement room, thereby enabling the person receiving the attunement to receive energies and blessings specific to him or her.

Healing Stubborn Blocks with the Angels

Often, it so happens that an underlying issue needs a deep healing through a conscious intervention before Reiki can balance stuck energies in specific locations of the energy field. In such cases, the angels can be of great assistance in helping us heal those underlying issues.

Whenever there are stubborn blocks to be healed, I invoke the angels (especially Archangels Michael and Raphael) and ask for their assistance in healing those blocks. If the energy seems to be stuck because of etheric cords between people, I request Archangel Michael to step forward and cut the cords. Once the cords are cut, the Reiki healing continues as usual and the area where the cords were cut is filled with Reiki. Once an area is healed fairly well with Reiki, I request Archangel Raphael to surround the area in his emerald green light in order to heal any residues that may be present.

Healing Personal Issues with the Angels

The best part about connecting with the angels is that we can share everything about our lives with them, without fear of being judged or ridiculed!

Whenever something bothers me, I write or type a letter to the angels and express my feelings to them. I know they listen each time because immediately after writing the letter, I feel a sense of peace. I feel deeply that the issue is now taken care of and I just have to let go and relax. And the issue is always taken care of and help from the angelic kingdom comes in varied ways!

The Angels as Our Friends

From my work with the angels, I have realised that the angels are absolutely unconditional beings who accept and love us exactly as we are. We don't have to pretend or strive to be different to receive their love. Not only do they accept us as we are, but they also help us heal our lives in the most magical of ways. They help us see and appreciate the divinity within us, even when we feel poorly about ourselves. The angels are my best friends because I can be myself with them! I can talk to them like I talk to a friend and expect their unconditional support and love.

The angels can be your friends too and assist in every area of your life. They can help you with your Reiki practice, they can guide you as you practise self healing or go about healing others, they can comfort you when you feel low and they can be by your side at all times. All you need to do is just ask. Ask and they will be there. And you will be surprised to find that they are among the sweetest of friends you could ever have! Angelic blessings to you.

Ten Signs from the Angels

All forms of energy healing share a connection in ways that are not always obvious. The energy of the angelic realm compliments the energy of Reiki. The angels are pure energy forms of love and light. They love connecting with Reiki healers. It usually happens that the angels come looking for us first rather than vice-versa.

If connecting with the angels happens to be part of your life's purpose, here are a few signs that may help you discover if the angels are reaching out to you.

1. As a child, were you *fascinated with angels and fairies*? If yes, it is a sign that the angels are part of your life. To quote my own example, no one in my family connected with the angels. Most didn't even believe in them. But I always felt a deep fascination for them. When my sister and I role played as children, I often played the role of an angel. The word *'angel'* sounded melodious to my ears! I also loved dressing up like an angel and singing angel songs.

2. You *feel naturally connected with the angelic realm* though you may not have all the information about it. You reach out to the angels in your own way.

3. You are inclined to *learning about angel healing*.

4. You *feel a sense of peace when you hear someone talking about the angels*, read about the angels or see angel pictures.

5. You often *sense warm energy near you*. This energy, which often signifies the presence of an angel, feels comforting to you.

6. You have *dreams and third eye visions of angels*. This is especially significant when you have these visions out of the blue rather than after you've read something related to the subject.

7. You *feel a fascination for crystals and colours*. The energy of every archangel is associated with the energy of a specific crystal. Feeling attracted to a crystal may signify that the corresponding archangel is trying to reach out to you.

8. You *stumble upon feathers* in unexpected locations.

9. After praying for help, you often *witness the sudden appearance of birds, butterflies and certain animals*. Seeing them gives you feelings of peace and reassurance. The angels often appear in different forms and bring us messages and healing.

10. *People often use the word 'angel' to address you* (especially when they don't believe in angels themselves)! This is because people are able to pick up the energy of the angels in your energy field, even if they are not consciously aware of it.

If you resonate with any of these, it is almost a certainty that the angels are part of your life, even if you were not conscious of it all these years. But now that you know the signs, trust that the angels are part of your life. You can start connecting with them right away. The more you connect, the stronger their presence becomes in your life and in your Reiki practice. For this, all you need to do is talk to the angels or write a letter to them. You can use the following lines as a reference and change the wording to suit your personal style.

"My Dear Angels, I wish to connect more with you. Please connect with me in whatever way is best for me. Thank you for being in my life."

Thereafter, let go and allow the angels to work their magic in your life. Enjoy connecting with the Angels!

Setting and Fulfilling Intentions with Reiki and Archangel Michael

When we desire something, the first thing we need to do is set an intention.

Often, our intentions are not strong enough. When this is the case, we end up sending mixed signals to the Universe. It is no wonder then that desires that are not backed by strong intentions take longer to manifest. We will have to struggle and stress ourselves a lot more when our intentions are not strong and clear.

One of the primary reasons for the inability to set clear intentions is that we often feel undeserving of what we desire. Many of us are conditioned to believe that life involves plenty of sacrifice and hardship and that an amazing life is the privilege of a chosen few. This is a self-limiting belief that can make life boring and hard.

The first thing we need to be aware of is that everyone deserves to have a good life. No matter how a person appears on the surface, deep down he carries the same light in him as the one carried by a Saint or other Higher Being. Every single soul is a child of the Universe. People make mistakes, go through hardships and face challenges in order to learn life lessons and balance karmas. However, no one is less deserving because of who he is or what he might have done in the past.

So, before you set an intention, it is crucial that you first change any self limiting beliefs you may have about your right to deserve. To aid this shift, we can use written affirmations. Start by writing a page of the following affirmations in a journal every day. You can either write all of them or choose one that you resonate most with.

1. *I am a child of the Universe. I deserve to enjoy all the good that life has to offer.*
2. *I deserve to have all of my heartfelt desires fulfilled.*
3. *I open my arms to receive all that I have asked for. I truly deserve it.*

After writing a page of this affirmation, draw the Reiki symbols Hon Sha Ze Sho Nen, Sei Hei Ki, and Cho Ku Rei anywhere on the page. You can draw as many as you feel like. Give Reiki to the page. This will help strengthen your new positive belief and also heal any feelings of not deserving that may be buried deep in your subconscious. You could also write or say the following prayer to connect with Archangel Michael and take his assistance to heal self limiting beliefs.

"Dear Archangel Michael,

Please help me feel the truth of my own divine light. Please help me to see that I am a child of the Universe and that I deserve to have all my desires fulfilled. I request you to clear and heal all the self limiting beliefs that I carry in my subconscious. Thank you."

Once you are clear about the fact that you deserve and have absorbed this new positive belief, start working on your intentions. Keep these pointers in mind as you work on your intentions.

1. Writing is extremely powerful when it comes to intentions. Write your intention down in a journal. Write it in the present tense. Draw the Reiki symbols on the page and give Reiki to it once every day.

2. Visualise how you would feel or what you would be doing if the intention has already manifested. For example, if your intention is to conceive and give birth to a child, visualise how it would feel to be carrying that baby and also to hold him or her in your arms after the birth. Visualise the details of the pregnancy and birth and make everything extremely positive. Feel it like it is happening now.

3. If you feel any discomfort or fear as you set your intentions, call upon Archangel Michael for help. Talk to him and express your fears. His warrior-like energies will help heal any blocks that you may be holding with respect to fulfilling your desires. If you are unable to pinpoint the exact fear, call upon Archangel Michael just before falling asleep. Ask him to work on your fears and blocks as you sleep. When we are asleep, our rational mind is at rest and we are naturally more open to healing. Do this every night until you feel extremely comfortable with your intentions.

4. Once your intentions are set, do not worry about how they will manifest. Take any action that you need to in order to manifest your intention and then let go. Remember your intentions have been charged with Reiki. Reiki is an intelligent energy and we do not have to instruct it on how it should go about fulfilling our desires. It knows exactly how to manifest our desires and also the timing in which to manifest them. Set the intention, give positive energy to it every day and then let it go. If you begin to feel anxious about the manifestation, call upon Archangel Michael again and request him to help you let go.

Strong intentions produce clear results. ALWAYS! And with the loving unconditional support of Reiki and Archangel Michael, you will be well on your way towards living your desires.

Healing Fear with Reiki and Archangel Michael

What is your greatest fear? What makes your heart beat fast, your hands sweaty and your mind spin? What triggers your anxiety?

Almost everyone has at least a couple of fears. Some fears are small, while others are big and strong. The strong fears are infused with a power so great that they overpower even the strongest and sanest of folks. A person who is normally composed can turn into a nervous wreck when in the grip of fear. Rationality and logic vanish and no amount of reassurance from people helps.

As a child, my greatest fear was that I would lose my mother. I had an irrational and almost obsessive fear of losing her. It was so strong that I would cry in fear if she travelled without me or left me alone with other family, especially at night. This fear of losing a loved one is quite common among people.

Some other common fears include:

- Fear of death
- Fear of illness
- Fear of being harmed
- Fear of darkness
- Fear of travelling
- Fear of failure
- Fear of ghosts
- Fear of abandonment
- Fear of flying

This list is practically endless. If you ask everyone you know about their fears, you will come across a variety of fears, some of which you can't even connect with! But that is the nature of fear. It is most often irrational and imaginary. This is different from the kind of fear you feel when faced with a truly dangerous situation. However, being in dangerous situations is certainly not an everyday occurrence.

This kind of logical thinking does not stop us from being fearful! So, how can we help ourselves when we stand face to face with our fears?

Here is a technique that can help you when you find yourself in the grip of irrational fear:

1. Sit or lie down comfortably.

2. Close your eyes and take a few deep breaths.

3. Feel your fear in all its intensity. Do not be afraid of feeling the fear. For instance, if you are afraid of an illness, feel the fear and all the scary details your mind projects about this illness. Don't worry, this will not manifest the illness. Since the intention behind feeling the fear is to release the energy associated with it, know that you are safe.

4. Now bring your awareness to your body. In which part of your body do you feel the effects of this fear? Do you feel tightness in your solar plexus or chest? Or do you feel heaviness in your head?

5. Once you locate the part of the body in which the fear manifests, place one of your palms on that part.

6. Give a shape and colour to this fear. Go with the first image that comes to your mind. Do not analyse. View this image in your mind's eye.

7. Now stretch your other hand, with the palm facing up. Request Archangel Michael or any other Spirit Guide you are comfortable working with to place their palm in yours.

8. Feel the powerful energy emanating from this fearless being. Breathe in and absorb some of his energy.

9. Now feel the power of your own being. You are inherently powerful. The scary voice in your head that makes you feel weak and fearful is the voice of the Ego.

10. With this awareness of your power, see yourself blowing the symbols Hon Sha Ze Sho Nen, Sei Hei Ki, and Cho Ku Rei to the image of the fear you hold in your mind's eye. Third level practitioners can also use the Master Symbol.

11. See the symbols flying towards the image of the fear and attaching themselves to it. See the fear being enveloped in Reiki and being transmuted into power and love.

12. Do this for as long as you feel like. If you feel weak or powerless while in the midst of the process, remind yourself that Archangel Michael (or your Spirit Guide) is with you. What is there to fear when you are in the company of such

powerful beings? They are there to assist you and help you recognise your own power. So, take their help.

13. Once you feel peaceful, thank Reiki and Archangel Michael (or your Spirit Guide) for their assistance.

Do this process whenever you find yourself in the grip of irrational fear. It may need to be done several times, often over months, before the fear is healed fully. You may also receive intuitive messages about other steps you can take to help with the healing. Cord cutting is particularly useful to heal deep-rooted fears.

If the fear overwhelms you to such an extent that you cannot even lie still and relax to do this process, it would be wise to work with a competent Reiki Master. Once the fear is at least partially healed and you feel comfortable, you can start working independently.

Your fears can be healed. You are much more powerful than any fearful projection of your Ego. You just have forgotten how powerful you are and it is now time for you to remember it!

Cord Cutting with Reiki and Archangel Michael

As we go about our lives, we form energetic cords with various people and situations. These cords keep us confined to unhealthy patterns that rob us of precious energy. We may have formed several cords over years (and lifetimes) without any awareness that we were doing this. But hereafter, we can choose to pay attention the minute we become aware that we are forming cords and nip it in the bud. Prevention is always better than cure.

Cord cutting is a powerful tool used by energy healers to chop off energy draining cords. It can be a rather intense experience and you may benefit by taking the assistance of your *Reiki Guides* and *Archangel Michael* during the process. It can be used to cut cords that have been around for eons of time and also to cut cords that are just beginning to grow. In case of cords that have been present for long periods of time, it might take several attempts before all cords are cut. Subsequently, the cords may grow back if there is something more that needs to be healed. So, keep working at it and always follow your inner guidance about how you must go about it. The following procedure only offers basic guidelines on cord cutting. It does not work the same way for everyone or even every time for the same individual. Use this as a reference but always remember to go with the flow and modify it as per how your process unfolds.

The Procedure

1. Purify your healing space by burning some incense and drawing the Reiki symbols on the walls and everywhere else that you feel guided to.

2. Light a white or violet coloured candle. Play some soothing music if you wish.

3. Sit before the candle and look into its light for two minutes. This light represents the truth of your Being- your Higher Self. Let your Higher Self be your guide as you embark on this process of healing.

4. In this meditative space, make a request as follows: *"My Dear Reiki Guide and Archangel Michael, please come to me now and assist me with this process of cord cutting and healing. Thank you."*

5. Wait until you sense the energy of the Higher Beings by your side. Trust the impressions you receive.

6. Now focus your attention on the person (or situation) with which you have cords attached. Feel any emotions that come up. Feel it as intensely as you need to. You are safe and

protected in the light of the Higher Beings and your own Higher Self.

7. Take a moment to locate that part of your body from which you sense these cords stemming. They are very often found stemming from the heart, solar plexus and third eye chakra. But they can be found in other areas as well. You may also find them stemming from multiple areas, in which case you will notice multiple cords. You must trust all the impressions you receive without stopping to analyse them logically.

8. Put out your dominant hand out and ask your Reiki guide to bless it. Visualise your hand turning into an energetic Reiki sword. You may also draw the symbols on the sword. And use it to chop off the energy cords that you previously located. As each cord is cut, visualise or intend that it drops into the light of the candle or to the ground and transforms into light.

9. Go slow and take the time to cut each cord that shows up. As you cut, you may find that more cords emerge. Continue to cut them. If you begin to feel overwhelmed, take a break, drink some water and request Michael to step in for you.

10. Lie still and allow Michael to chop off the remainder of the cords with his own energy sword. This is a deeply healing experience. As the cords are cut, you may also get a sense of how the cords feel. Some cords feel sticky, while others feel slushy. Some feel dense, while others feel like threads.

11. As the cords are cut, you are likely to feel various bodily sensations. You may also feel a sense of relief, relaxed, emotional etc.

12. For the final few cords, it would be good for you to get back in action again. Use your Reiki sword of light to chop them off and let them all go.

13. Now lie still for a few minutes and request your Reiki Guide and Archangel Michael to fill you up with divine healing energy. You may also request several guides and angels to work on you and to heal the areas that were most affected by these cords.

14. Finally, express your gratitude to Reiki, your Reiki guide, Michael and to everything and everyone else who facilitated this healing for you.

15. Give yourself a pat on the back for having made an empowering choice in life.

16. Drink lots of water, relax and enjoy the feelings of freedom and liberation that this exercise brings!

Build Your Healing Practice with Archangel Michael

Are you aware of your life's purpose? What is your calling? What special gifts do you have that you can share with the world?

If you are a Reiki practitioner, Reiki is something you may wish to share with the world. Are you doing justice to your Reiki practice and to all your other gifts? If not, what is holding you back?

Several healers feel a calling from the depths of their heart. They can vaguely remember what they came here to do. They are aware that they have innate healing abilities with which they can make a difference. However, they feel stuck on their path. Does that sound like you? That was me too, some years ago.

Right through my college days and a subsequent six years in another career, something didn't feel right about what I was doing with my life. I had a hard time figuring out what that "something" was. All I knew was that I was not happy with the academic courses I did or the jobs I worked at. People thought I was an idealist on the lookout for a perfect career. But I knew deep down that I was not looking for an ideal set up. I knew I had a different purpose to fulfill and it just took time for me to figure out what that purpose was.

The purpose was actually unfolding all along. All the experiences I had and the challenges I faced before and even after I became a Reiki practitioner helped me reach where I am today. Being determined about my life's path and not being swayed by others' opinions helped immensely.

The good news is that you can do it too! You can follow your heart and fulfil your purpose. You can use your healing abilities and teach others about it too. You can create a life that feels meaningful to you and which satisfies the longing of your soul. All you need is a strong will and a bit of courage.

Take Small Steps Each Day

If you wish to have an independent Reiki or spiritual teaching practice, start moving in the direction of your dreams today. Maybe you can't afford to quit your current job and set up a full time Reiki practice right away. But you can certainly accomplish a little bit each day. If you wish to do more healing work and you don't have clients and students yet, heal with Reiki in other ways. You may have a garden at home. Why not give Reiki to your plants? If you have pets at home, why not pamper them with Reiki treatments? Give Reiki to Planet Earth and play a role in its healing. And most important of all, heal yourself with Reiki every day. Remember, the more you heal yourself, the more you are able to help others heal. These may seem like small steps but they can go a long way in helping you fulfil your life's purpose. With every small step you take, you inspire the Universe to take ten steps more. And you will soon find yourself living life at your highest potential.

Call on Archangel Michael

You can also call on Archangel Michael to help you move ahead on your life's path. Michael loves to help healers and spiritual teachers fulfil their purpose. The best way to connect with Michael is to have a personal interaction with him.

This is one technique you may want to try:

1. Go outdoors in nature (preferably in your own private garden or roof terrace). If that is not feasible, don't worry. You can do it indoors too.

2. Take a few deep breaths and relax. Call upon Archangel Michael and request him to be by your side. Call him from your heart.

3. When you call on Michael, you can be certain that he will be there. You may feel a warm presence beside you or you may just sense that he is by your side. Once you intuitively sense that Michel is beside you, hold his hand. If you ask for your hand to be held, rest assured that it will be held (even if you can't feel it). Or you may find that Michael puts his arm around you. Trust your intuition and go with the flow. Stroll around your garden with him. Walking with Archangel Michael is like walking with a wise old friend and sharing your life's story with him along the way!

4. Pour your heart out to Michael. Talk to him loudly (if possible), as it can help you connect better. No one is around to judge you or laugh at you. Tell him about your desires and aspirations with regards to your life's purpose. Tell him about your fears and about everything that is holding you back. Ask him to guide you.

5. Notice all the empowering thoughts and feelings that enter your awareness as you walk. These are Michael's messages for you. If you receive a message that does not feel right, know that it is coming from the Ego and not from Michael. The angels always give us empowering messages, even when the messages have challenging guidance. Trust your intuition and accept only those messages that feel right.

6. Thank the Archangel for his guidance and request him to continue helping you with your life's purpose.

Just the act of walking with Archangel Michael will help you feel powerful. It can help you develop a strong will and to become your own Master and guide. His messages serve as additional guidance.

There is no better time to start than now. Do whatever you can to fulfil your life's purpose today, no matter how small the step. And allow Archangel Michael to be your mentor. Do you know how blessed we are to have angelic guides and mentors?

Be fearless and know that you can accomplish your life's purpose. You can be an amazing Reiki healer, a powerful spiritual teacher and everything else that will make a difference to you and to the world!

Safety and Protection with Archangel Michael

There are times when all of us experience feelings of being unsafe. In such moments, we allow our thoughts to rein over us and create monsters that scare the hell out of us. These monsters are usually of our own making but it is hard to see this truth when gripped by fear.

Feelings of fear and lack of safety are all vibrations in our energy field. We have the power to heal them by connecting with the part of us that is well grounded, safe and free from fear.

The energies of the mighty Archangel Michael resonate with strength and courage. Michael represents that aspect of Source (or God) that reflects safety, strength, purity and courage. By connecting with Michael, we allow the same aspect in us to grow stronger. In addition, we can use the Reiki symbols.

Here are some ways that you can invoke protection and gain strength whenever you feel unsafe.

Chanting/ Singing

The moment you notice feelings of being unsafe taking over you, chant or sing Michael's name and connect with his energy. This is not done as worship. The intention is to connect with Michael's energy and to thereby get in touch with the aspect in us that represents courage and strength.

Home Protection

If you ever feel unsafe at home, either because you live alone or because you have other kinds of irrational fears, you can call on Michael to watch over your home. This is especially powerful when done before bedtime. It can help you sleep in peace. Just before drifting off to sleep, call on Michael and request him to surround your house with his presence. Visualise him standing at the front door and at the back door. Then visualise him standing by the left of your house and also on the right. You will be able to sense his powerful energy envelop your house. Give thanks and fall asleep in peace.

Outside Protection

If you are travelling or going to a place that makes you feel unsafe, request Michael to accompany you. All you need to do is say these words before you get going. *"Dear Archangel Michael, please accompany me. Please protect me and help me feel safe. Thank you for your presence."* You can also do this when you find yourself walking or driving alone in an isolated place. You can do this on an aeroplane if flying makes you nervous. You may sense a warm presence beside you or just know that Michael is with you. Irrespective of whether you feel anything or not, calling on Michael will bring his energy to your side. All you need to do is trust.

Protection for Children

Children are often afraid of darkness, monsters and the like. But the good thing is that they are also more receptive to divine energies when compared to adults. Let your children know about Archangel Michael. Show them some pictures of Michael from the internet or from your set of oracle cards. Tell them that they can call on Michael any time they feel afraid and that he will be right there to take care of them. If it is a younger child, you can call on Michael on the child's behalf. Do this loudly so the child hears what you are saying and feels reassured. If your children are older and have begun to move around independently, you can request Michael to accompany them and to keep them safe.

Symbol Protection

Apart from calling on Michael, you can also invoke the Reiki symbols. Third degree practitioners can visualise the symbol Dai Ko Myo in front of them. Dai Ko Myo represents truth, light and power. Visualise it over your house at night. Visualise it surrounding your house on all four sides. Second-degree practitioners can use Sei He Ki or all three symbols. Chant the names of the symbols for a deeper connection. First-degree practitioners can just visualise a blanket of Reiki enveloping them, their house, vehicle etc.

May the energy of Archangel Michael be with you always.

Reiki Psychic Surgery with Archangel Raphael

Psychic surgery is high-level energy work. Generally speaking, it is recommended that only third degree practitioners with sufficient experience do this. If you have not done the third degree yet but are highly intuitive and skilled with energy work, you can consult with your higher self and then decide if you should do it or not.

Psychic surgery can be done to heal stubborn blocks that do not respond to gentler healing. It is commonly done to treat physical ailments but it can work for mental-emotional issues as well. Reiki psychic surgery involves using several healing techniques in conjunction with Reiki and the power of your intuition.

This article explains Reiki psychic surgery as done under the guidance of Archangel Raphael. Raphael is the Master-Healer of the angelic realm and he takes delight in helping Reiki healers. In order to provide maximum benefit to yourself or your client, you must be able to put your logical mind aside and trust your intuition one hundred percent. When you surrender completely, Raphael works beautifully through you and the whole process feels effortless. Raphael plays the role of chief surgeon who is around to help and guide. We play the role of assistant surgeons who are training under him!

Who needs Psychic Surgery? Risks vs Benefits

Psychic surgery is normally done only when nothing else seems to help. It is not necessary in all cases and can cause uncomfortable symptoms if done for no reason. Doctors perform a caesarean section only when the baby's position does not allow a natural birth or labour does not progress as expected. Surgery done for no reason can cause more harm than good. So, put on a medical hat and assess the risks and benefits of performing psychic surgery. If the benefits outweigh the risks, go ahead! If they don't, stick with gentler healing.

The Procedure

1. Prepare the healing area by physically cleaning it. Cleanse the room by drawing Dai Ko Myo and Cho Ku Rei on the walls, ceiling, floor, the healing couch/massage table and everywhere else that you feel guided to.

2. Place a picture (or oracle card) of Archangel Raphael and other Masters, Guides and Angels that you connect with.

3. Light candles, burn some incense and play soothing music.

4. Have plenty of water handy.

5. Take a few deep breaths and centre yourself. Request Raphael to help you with this process and to perform the surgery through you. Request your guides and angels to surround you in a shield of protective light so as to keep your energies safe.

6. Ask your client to come in and lie down. Begin by scanning the aura and make a note of the areas where the energy feels stuck or heavy.

7. Encourage your client to locate areas where energies feel stubbornly stuck.

8. If it is a specific organ or body part that needs healing, you will still need to scan the aura and locate the areas that hold stubborn blocks. This is because stuck energies are not always restricted to a diseased body part. They are usually present in several areas of the body and each one must be addressed independently for a full healing to occur.

9. Once you identify the areas that have stuck energies, call on Archangel Raphael and ask him to guide every move of yours as you go about performing the surgery.

10. In the case of physical ailments, also scan the diseased body part or organ for stuck energies.

11. Assess the nature of every stubborn block you encounter. Does the block feel rough and hard? Does it feel icky and soft? Does it feel coarse? What shape does it have? What colour is it? Trust the impressions you first receive. Depending on the nature of the block, proceed to remove it. Use the Violet Flame to transmute the blocks. The energy that is removed can be tossed into the Violet Flame where it will be transmuted.

12. A block that feels hard may need to be drilled or extracted. A block that feels icky may need to be cut. Cut, drain, repair and stitch as a surgeon would do. Move your hands exactly like you would if you were a surgeon performing surgery. You must literally play around with the energy. With Archangel Raphael acting as your guide, you cannot make a mistake.

13. Take breaks in between and drink water. Same goes for your client.

14. If something feels overwhelming, take a break. Sit down, drink some water and relax. Request Archangel Raphael to work on your client while you rest. Watch what happens and observe how Raphael works. You may learn a thing or two. Get back to working alongside Raphael when you feel ready.

15. It is not necessary for all blocks to be cleared in one session. When you intuitively feel that you must stop for the day, feel free to stop. It is good to give the body time to adjust with the healing that occurred. Do not force healing beyond what is necessary at the moment.

16. It is important to fill up the areas that were worked on with healing energy. Request Raphael to direct his healing green light through your palms. Fill up all the areas that were worked on with this green light and intend that it stays there for as long as necessary.

17. Proceed to do a full body healing with Reiki, paying special attention to the areas that were worked on. If any of the chakras seem deficient in energy, strengthen them with balls of light of the corresponding chakra colours. For

example, if the root chakra needs extra attention, make an energy ball of red light and push it into the chakra. This must be done alongside the Reiki healing.

18. Once done, wrap the client in a cocoon of Reiki/emerald green light/white light/pink light (as you feel guided to). Draw the Master and power symbols on the cocoon and seal the healing.

19. Request Raphael to stay by the client's side for as long as necessary and to keep him or her comfortable.

20. If the client is asleep, leave him or her undisturbed.

21. Drink plenty of water and get your client to do the same once he or she wakes up.

Post Healing Discussion

Encourage your client to take further action steps towards healing the root cause of the issue. Every disease and imbalance has an underlying root cause. And until we take steps to heal the root cause, it is quite likely that the blocks will resurface. If the case has been thoroughly discussed earlier, you may be aware of the root cause already. Alternately, you may receive information about the root cause during the healing. If you need further assistance, you can do angel card readings to receive specific guidance for your client. Discuss your findings with the client and guide him or her on further action steps.

Cleansing

Since a lot of negative energy is released during psychic surgery, it is important that the healing area is cleansed thoroughly before you use it again. Burn some incense and allow its smoke to permeate every corner of the room. Allow it to touch the area where the client lay down. Draw the Master Symbol and Power Symbol once again on the walls, ceiling, floor, door, windows etc. Place balls of Reiki in each corner of the room. Toss one huge ball into the centre of the room to keep the energy flowing.

Reiki and Archangel Haniel

Archangel Haniel has a lovely energy that resonates with the moon. The crystal associated with her is moonstone. She can help us when we feel sensitive and out of balance. Working with her may be particularly helpful to women who find themselves going off balance at varied times of the menstrual cycle. If you are a woman and you face this problem every month, you can connect with Archangel Haniel. Haniel's soft energy can ease hormonal fluctuations and help you maintain a state of harmony and balance. This apart, she also helps anyone who feels sensitive, unworthy/unlovable and out of balance in general (men included).

The best time to work with Archangel Haniel is during the time of the full moon. But you don't have to wait for the full moon to connect with her. You can also call on her at other times and she will be happy to help you. Using or wearing a moonstone crystal can help you connect with her energies better.

Healing with Reiki and Moonstone

1. Ensure your moonstone crystal has been cleaned and cleared of all negative energies.

2. Hold the crystal between your palms and charge it with Reiki for a while.

3. Call upon Archangel Haniel and ask her to bless this stone with her energy.

4. Request Archangel Haniel to sit beside you as you prepare to heal yourself with Reiki.

5. Begin to do a full body Reiki healing.

6. As you heal yourself, place the moonstone crystal on whatever chakra or part of the body that you are guided to. Trust your intuition and feel free to move it around. You will not make a mistake when you trust your feelings.

7. You can also request Archangel Haniel to heal you with her energies and just relax as the energies work on you.

This act of receiving from Haniel will help you understand that it is OK to receive in life. A lot of energetic imbalances occur when we become perpetual givers and also when we try to be in control at all times. We must also learn to receive and to let go of control at times. This helps our energies stay in harmony and balance.

Full Moon Healing with Archangel Haniel

1. Go outdoors on the evening of the full moon. Your own garden, balcony or roof terrace would work best. If that is not feasible, you can do it indoors in a space that offers you a view of the full moon.

2. Take a few deep breaths to relax and center yourself.

3. Call on Archangel Haniel. Say, *"Dear Archangel Haniel, Please be with me now and help me heal."*

4. Look at the full moon and visualise Archangel Haniel standing behind it.

5. Intend that the energies from Haniel and the moon wash over you from head to toe and bring balance to your body, mind and spirit.

6. Bask in this energy for as long as you like.

7. Once done, thank Haniel and the moon for their help.

8. Drink plenty of water.

This meditation can also be done when the full moon is not around. All you need to do is visualise a full moon and proceed to heal yourself as described above.

Enjoy feeling balanced and harmonious!

Live Your Passions and Create a Colourful Life with Reiki and Archangel Haniel

What are you passionate about in life? How many of your passions are you living? Are you aware of your passions? I would like to share my list of passions.

I am passionate about:
1. Life
2. Music
3. Dance
4. Healing
5. Energy work
6. Teaching others about healing, energy work and angels
7. Angel card readings
8. Reading
9. Writing
10. Nurturing my child
11. Romance and love
12. Good food
13. Travel

14. Rest and Relaxation
15. Spiritual Growth and learning
16. Nature
17. Pampering myself and my inner child
18. Spending time by myself

Exercise

Before you read further, take a pen and paper and make a list of all the things that you are passionate about.

We may add more things to the list as life goes by. Passion does not always involve "big" stuff. You can even be passionate about relishing a cup of tea. It is perfectly normal to be passionate about the small things in life. Ultimately, it is those small things that determine the quality of our lives on a day to day basis.

Now look at the list of passions that you have made. Spend some time reflecting on all that you have written. How many of your passions are you living? Are you satisfied with what you see? Or would you like to add more colour to your life by living your passions on a day to day basis?

It takes **courage** to live your passions because it often involves being criticized or misunderstood by family and friends. Everyone does not understand our passions and may not be fully supportive of us living our passions. ***But life is meant to be lived fully.*** Every day can be so full of joy and meaning, if only we could allow our passions to lead us. So, the first thing to do is to decide that you will dedicate at least some time everyday to living at least one of your passions. If your family is supportive of this, good for you! If not, you will need to have a heart to heart conversation with them and explain why this is important to you. Most people understand when something is communicated to them respectfully. For instance, you may feel the need to spend some time alone everyday to just be by yourself. If you have never expressed this need of yours in the past, it may come as a surprise to those closest to you. Nevertheless, if it is on your list of passions, you will benefit if you give yourself that time alone every day. When you give yourself the permission to do this, it means you love yourself and like to take care of yourself. And when you take good care of yourself, you also end up taking good care of the people close to you.

The following pointers can guide you as you work on living your passions and making your life more meaningful.

Make the Time

Allocate time slots in your weekly schedule to live your passions- it could be an hour every day, a few hours every week or one day in a week, as per your convenience. It would be ideal if you could devote some time to at least a couple of your passions every day. But if that is not possible, make sure you at least dedicate one day a week to living your passions.

Chart/Vision Board

Collect pictures that reflect your passions from newspapers and magazines. Stick all the pictures on a chart or board and hang the chart in a place where it is easily visible to you during the course of the day. You can even draw the Reiki symbols on the chart if you wish to. Looking at this chart will inspire you to live your passions!

Reiki and Archangel Haniel

Give Reiki to your list of passions and to your chart whenever possible. This will add energy to your passions and make them a lot more powerful.

You can also take the help of Archangel Haniel to live your passions, especially when you need to take risks to do so. For example, someone who is initially passionate about an activity may, over time, feel a strong calling to convert this passion into a full time career. When this happens, the person may have to take certain risks and move past comfort zones. However, when something is felt as a true calling, it is meant to be part of our life's plan and purpose. And we are sure to receive support from the Universe as we make life changes to accommodate our passions. However, the only requirement is that we ask for help. When you feel afraid or unsure about living a passion of yours or about moving past your comfort zone, call upon Archangel Haniel. Haniel whose name means "Glory of God" can help you use your potential to the fullest and make your transition into the unknown comfortable.

When we were children, we were naturally tuned into our passions and naturally believed that life was a joyous experience meant to be lived passionately. As we grew older, we were conditioned to believe that life is a struggle. As a result, many of us developed the belief that having fun and living passionately is something meant only for the young. Nothing could be further from the truth. Age is just a number and has absolutely nothing to do with living your passions or having fun. The spirit of the child that you once were is still alive in you. All you need to do is recognise it and set it free. Once you set it free, this childlike presence in you will help you live all of your passions and make life a truly amazing journey!

Communication with Departed Loved Ones: Reiki and Archangel Azrael

Archangel Azrael is known as "The Angel of Death." He helps souls cross over comfortably to the other side. He also helps these souls communicate with near and dear ones on Earth. People who are alive can also take his assistance to establish communication with the souls of their departed loved ones.

As Reiki practitioners, we have the added benefit of using Reiki along with help from Archangel Azrael. Reiki energy being soft and loving creates a safe and peaceful space for soul communication to happen.

This kind of communication should only be done only to express such things that would help us and also help the souls of our loved ones. Positive and kind words that were unexpressed when the person was alive can certainly be expressed. Asking for forgiveness for any pain we caused them and sending our love is also perfectly fine.

In short, any message that comes from the heart is good. Love is the key.

If what you wish to convey is not coming from a place of love (that is, it is coming from the Ego), don't express it. Your intuition will guide you.

Here is a brief outline of the process:

1. Keep a piece of paper and pen with you.

2. Sit in a quiet place where you will be left undisturbed.

3. You can play soothing music and also light a candle if it helps.

4. Take a few deep breaths and get into a meditative state.

5. Visualise the room being flooded with Reiki. You can also draw any symbols that you are guided to in the air.

6. Bring your awareness to your heart. You can place your palm on the heart to connect with it. What message of love does your heart wish to send to the soul of your loved one? Start writing the message on the piece of paper. Keep your words positive and loving.

7. Give Reiki to this piece of paper. This will strengthen the element of love in your message.

8. Call upon Archangel Azrael. If you work with angel card decks, pick any card of Archangel Azrael from the deck to connect with him. If you wish to, you can also place the card along with your piece of paper. Request him to take this message to your loved one.

9. You can also request Azrael to bring a message back to you from your loved one.

10. Express your gratitude to the Archangel for his assistance.

11. Put the piece of paper away in a safe place.

12. Thereafter, notice any messages you may receive from the other side. These messages may come in the form of feelings- you may feel a deep sense of peace or you may feel a surge of love. Unhealed feelings that you may have carried about your past relationship with this person are suddenly healed. You may also receive messages in the form of words that you read somewhere or as songs that play on the radio or television. It may also be in the form of visits from certain animals or birds. Each one's experience is unique. You will know it is a message for you when you receive it.

13. Do not analyse the message by allowing your logical mind to kick in. Trust your feelings and accept the message you get.

14. Once you have received your message, discard the paper by either burning or burying it.

This technique is particularly useful when we wish to express love and forgiveness to our departed loved ones. When people are alive, we sometimes take them for granted. We may also focus only on the negative aspects of their personality. And when the person is no more, we realise their value and also recognise their positive traits. This tends to bring up feelings of sadness and guilt in us. However, feeling sad or guilty does not help anyone. As we grow spiritually, it is important to remind ourselves constantly that the core of our being is pure love. Anything that is not love is not who we are. Due to our identification with the ego, all of us err from time to time. So, if you feel sad or guilty about something you did or did not do (or something you said or did not say) when a loved one was with you, it is not too late. It is possible to express your feelings even now. Rest assured that the power of love will heal everything that is unhealed in all of space and time and restore the flow of love in your relationship.

Chakra Clearing with Reiki and Archangel Metatron

I do Angel Card Readings every single day to receive guidance for my personal growth. For a period in time, I kept drawing the card of Archangel Metatron from the deck **'Archangels'** designed by Doreen Virtue. This card guided me to clear my chakras with his help. I did not take this guidance seriously and kept putting off working with Archangel Metatron for several days. But like all card readers would know, you keep drawing the same cards until you follow the guidance being given to you. I drew the card so many times that I finally decided to work with this mighty Archangel.

I learnt from the readings that Archangel Metatron heals with sacred geometric shapes and uses a tool that some refer to as a *"Metatron Cube"*. In order to facilitate healing, he passes his cube right through your energy body. The cube rotates as it moves through your energy field and clears toxins from each of your chakras.

When I finally used the Metatron cube to heal myself, I found the results to be quite amazing. I could feel the cube clearing away all toxic energies as it rotated. Since then I have begun to take the assistance of Archangel Metatron and his sacred cube during some Reiki healings that I know would benefit from this additional help.

If you have pressing issues with any of your chakras or would just like a thorough cleansing of all your chakras, you will benefit from working with Archangel Metatron as well. This technique can be easily incorporated with your daily routine of Reiki self healing. You will not need to use this technique every day. You can use it once every few days depending on the health of your chakras. Trust your intuition and use it when you feel like.

Here's how you go about it:

1. Take a deep breath.

2. Call upon Archangel Metatron to assist you with clearing your chakras. If you have an angel card of Metatron with you, you can place it close to you during the healing.

3. Visualise the Archangel and his cube. Do not worry too much about the visual details. Your intention to connect with the Archangel and his cube will ensure that you are connected.

4. Visualise the Archangel sending his cube towards the top of your head. Visualise the cube spinning inside your crown

chakra. Intuitively scan the chakra for traces of toxins. Feel these toxins being cleared by the spinning cube.

5. Next move to the third eye chakra and repeat the same process. Similarly, move the cube through each of the chakras and allow it to work on each one, thereby clearing every chakra of toxic debris.

6. Trust your intuition. Let the cube move as it wishes to. There is no strict rule to be followed as to which chakra must be cleared first. You may find the cube moving randomly from chakra to chakra and also moving back to do more work on chakras that were already cleared. Do not analyse. Just go with the flow and relax. You will not make a mistake when you trust your intuition.

7. Once you feel that you are done, thank the Archangel for his assistance with this healing.

8. Proceed to do a full body Reiki healing as usual.

9. Drink plenty of water.

There is no limit to the number of ways in which we can heal ourselves. It is always nice to experiment with different techniques and absorb the benefit that each technique has to offer. The beauty of Reiki lies in its flexibility. It can be incorporated with most other techniques and it works so beautifully. If you enjoy healing with the angels, you are sure to enjoy working with Archangel Metatron and his sacred cube!

Spiritual Power with Reiki, Raziel and Rainbow Energy

There is an interesting quote that says,

"We are not human beings having a spiritual experience. We are spiritual beings having a human experience" - Pierre Teilhard de Chardin.

From a limited perspective, we humans appear to be insignificant little beings in a mysterious cosmos that we cannot comprehend with our senses. This is the perspective of the human ego, which has grown accustomed to viewing everything and everyone as separate. This feeling of separation is the root cause of several problems on Earth. From the perspective of spirit, we all are just one energy form, which is seemingly split into multiple fragments. We are one with the whole Universe.

As spiritual beings, we are inherently powerful with the capacity to live amazing lives, love beyond measure and heal with power. But many of us feel like helpless victims being tossed around by forces beyond our control. We look for people and circumstances to blame when all we need to do is look within and connect with our true source of power. After having lived as powerless beings for so long, it can be rather difficult to reclaim our spiritual power in a jiffy. To make this task easier for us, we can call on Archangel Raziel.

Archangel Raziel is often referred to as the *"Wizard of the Archangel Realm"*. In pictures and oracle cards, he is often depicted as a wise old man with a beard. He is an embodiment of wisdom, power and knowledge. He is the Archangel to call on when we wish to understand the secrets of the Universe and our relationship with existence. He can help us master the art of manifestation. He can help us heal the third eye chakra and to develop the ability to see beyond what the senses show. He can help us tap into our innate healing powers and to remember what we already know in the depths of our being.

Healing with Archangel Raziel

1. Light a candle and play some soothing music.

2. Lie down comfortably.

3. Take a few deep breaths and centre yourself.

4. Request Archangel Raziel to be your guide and to sit by your side.

5. Visualise a beautiful rainbow over you. The light associated with Raziel as well as Reiki is rainbow coloured light. By visualising the rainbow, you will be making a connection with both.

6. Visualise this rainbow coloured light flowing down and enveloping you from head to toe. See yourself afloat on

waves of this rainbow energy and let it wash over you from every angle.

7. Visualise the Reiki symbols of your choice dropping down from the rainbow and working on you. Do use the Master Symbol if you've done third degree.

8. Just relax and allow the rainbow energy to work on you.

9. After a while, allow yourself to expand. See yourself as an energy form moving beyond the body and becoming one with the Universe.

10. Put your hand out and reach out to the mighty Raziel. Allow his energy to touch you. See yourself as wise and powerful, just like him. In the light of the rainbow, you are able to see your connection with all of existence and you get closer to Spirit, which is your true self.

11. Feel all the blocks in your third eye dissolving. As the blocks dissolve, allow your healing powers to resurface. If you are a Reiki healer in this lifetime, it is quite likely that you have been a powerful healer in some of your past lives too. You are a talented healer and you know much more than you think you do. Allow your talents to resurface.

12. Flow with the experience. Allow your intuition to lead you if you need additional healing with any issue that pops into your awareness at this point. You can visualise rainbow energy surrounding the situation and heal it from a place of power.

13. Stay in this state for as long as you wish to and absorb all the energy being sent your way. Once done, take a few

moments to relax and return to your normal state of awareness.

14. Thank Raziel and Reiki for their help.

This practice is best done before going to bed as the sleep state can help you absorb the healing faster. But it can be done at other times as well. The more you work with Archangel Raziel, the more you will open up to the power of your Being. You will understand the dynamics of the Universe and find true power as you discover your oneness with existence. You will master the art of manifestation. Instead of begging and pleading with the Universe to fulfil your desires, you will emerge as a powerful co-creator and become the scriptwriter of your destiny. You will acknowledge and appreciate your healing powers and use it for the greatest good of humanity.

Energy Clearing with Reiki and Archangel Jophiel

All of us tend to pick up negative energies from time to time. We come in contact with a variety of people, places and objects. Depending on our level of sensitivity, we tend to pick up negativities from the external world. Some people are more vulnerable to energies and pick them up faster while others are more resistant. These energies linger in our aura and can make us feel low. Our homes also pick up energies from visitors and from the vibrations that we and our family members emit. Reiki practice in itself helps to clear our energies to a large extent. This is one reason it is so important for us to practise Reiki every day. It helps to clear negativities from our aura on a daily basis thereby keeping our energies clean and pure.

An Archangel by name Jophiel can also help us clear away negativities from our bodies, auras as well as homes.

Here are some ways that we can work with Reiki and Archangel Jophiel:

1. Spend a few minutes every day or at least once a week in a place of nature. It could be a park, your garden, under a tree or even beside a potted plant in your balcony. Take a few deep breaths and connect with Archangel Jophiel. Request her to come to you and to help clear away all negative energies from your physical and energy bodies. Go for a walk or just be seated and relax while allowing Jophiel to work on you.

2. Call upon Jophiel during self Reiki sessions and request her to help you release all negative energies from your system. Before you begin draw a large power symbol in front of you. This symbol also assists with clearing negative energies.

3. Request Jophiel to assist with cleansing the energy of your home. If you cleanse your home with incense, ask Jophiel to accompany you to each of the rooms as you walk around and allow the smoke from the incense to touch your home. If you light candles or keep fresh flowers, request Jophiel to touch them with her energy, thereby bringing in more beauty and positive energy into your home.

4. Most importantly, request Jophiel to stay by your side and to help you clear your mind of unhelpful and energy draining thoughts and patterns. We often end up creating difficult situations in our lives because we aren't able to connect with our inner beauty, which is the light of our soul. If we can begin to connect with our inner beauty, it will radiate outward and have a positive impact on every aspect

of our lives. Jophiel can help you fall in love with your inner self!

The Power of the Violet Flame in Reiki Healing

If you have practised Reiki for a sufficiently long time, you will know that there are some problems and patterns that are highly stubborn. These could be physical, mental or emotional issues.

Often, just channeling Reiki is enough. The energy manages to set things right over time and brings the body back into a state of harmony and balance. However, there are some kinds of blocks that are highly stubborn and almost tend to resist any kind of an intervention. Such blocks could be compared with water pipes that are blocked due to obstructions of any kind. In such pipes, there is no way the water can flow freely until the block is removed.

In cases of stubborn patterns, the energy is like the water that is unable to flow freely until the block (physical/emotional/mental) is cleared from the energy field.

In such cases, the violet flame is a powerful tool that can come to our aid. The Violet Flame is associated with the seventh ray of spiritual light. It is said that, in the past, the power of the violet flame was known only to a few Ascended Masters and other Higher Beings. But in the New Age of today, its power is being made available to all those who are ready to work with it. Saint Germain is the Ascended Master responsible for making the power of the violet flame available to the world today.

The power of the violet flame ensures that it not only absorbs energetic patterns and debris from the aura, but it also transmutes them into light.

This technique of healing with the violet flame is particularly effective after one is attuned to the Master Degree. However, it can fetch results after other degrees as well (depending on how deeply connected the healer is to energy work). Many people who go on to do the Master Degree are highly sensitive to energy and they can literally play around with energy to heal! So, if you resonate with the idea of using the violet flame to heal stubborn patterns in yourself or others.

Here is how you can go about it:

1. Before you begin, request Archangel Michael to protect you. You can say something like, "Dear Archangel Michael, as I prepare to do this healing work, please surround me in your golden light and please protect me. Thank you."

2. Then call upon Archangel Raphael. You can say something like, "Dear Archangel Raphael, please assist me as I work towards healing these blocks. Please help me to

remove and clear these blocks from my (or client's) energy field. Thank you."

3. Call upon Saint Germain. You can say, "Dear Ascended Master, Saint Germain, please help me work and heal using the power of the violet flame. Thank you."

4. Take three deep breaths and prepare yourself for the healing.

5. Invoke the Violet Flame, "Dear Violet Flame, please receive all these blocks that I am going to pour into you and transmute them into pure divine light."

6. Imagine a violet fire burning in front of you. If imagining is difficult, you can also use a violet coloured candle and look at its flame as the violet flame.

7. Open up the fingers of your hand / hands.

8. If you wish to, imagine them being extended so they can reach the block easily.

9. Sense the energetic block in the body and start scooping it out with your fingers.

10. As you scoop it out pour the energetic debris into the violet flame. If you are using a candle, you will pour the debris over the visible flame of the candle.

11. As you pour the debris into the violet flame, you can visualise it being transmuted into light.

12. Do this process for as long as you feel like. Once you feel you have cleared enough for one session, you can stop.

13. Once you decide to stop, express your gratitude to the Violet Flame and to Saint Germain. It could go like, "Dear

Violet Flame and Ascended Master Saint Germain, please accept my gratitude for your assistance during this healing session. Thank you, thank you, thank you."

14. Now visualise the violet flame turning off. If you are using a candle, put it off.

15. Proceed to do a full body healing with Reiki, paying particular attention to the area that was treated with the violet flame. While treating that area, visualise it being flooded with Reiki. Also, visualise it being whole and healed.

16. Once you are done with the full body healing, express your gratitude to Reiki, Archangel Michael, Archangel Raphael and other higher beings you may have called upon to assist you with healing.

17. Drink lots of water and relax.

Notes:

1. Keep in mind that blocks that require the power of the violet flame may take time to heal. The bigger the block, the more the time. So, you might have to use the violet flame continuously for some sessions to achieve a full healing. This process can go on for a few days, a few months and occasionally even years.

2. This is a very high level of energy work and it can sometimes be followed by a healing crisis. It is recommended that you work with this only if you are very comfortable with energy work and can support yourself in the event of a healing crisis.

Guide to Archangels and Crystals

This is for everyone who likes working with angels and crystals.

Who are the Archangels?

The angelic realm is like a celestial workforce with varied departments. There are guardian angels, archangels, nature angels, romance angels/cherubs and many other categories of angels working together.

The Archangels belong to one department. Their energies are very pure and of a high vibration, resonating closely with the energies of Source or God. They each represent one aspect or quality of Source. By connecting with the archangels, we get in touch with the same qualities latent in us. We strengthen those aspects, thereby dropping layers of conditioning and negativity. We step outside the veil of amnesia and remember who we truly are. We recognise the light shining within us.

It is often misunderstood that the angels are around only to fulfill our wishes or to perform miracles in our lives. While it is true that wishes get fulfilled and miracles happen, it is not true that the angels do this for us. By connecting with angelic energies, we raise our vibration to a level, which enables us to live a life of miracles. The energy of the angels only acts as a medium for us to get in touch with that part of ourselves where everything is a possibility.

The table below provides a brief summary of fifteen archangels that I learnt about from the work of Doreen Virtue. Ever since, I have worked extensively with each of them both to heal myself and to help others heal. Every archangel is associated with a crystal. If you feel a connection with any of the archangels, you may benefit by working with the corresponding crystal. And if you are drawn to a particular crystal, you may enjoy working with the corresponding archangel!

The more you work with angels and crystals, the more you will discover their resonance with Reiki. You will also learn to seamlessly integrate one with the other. Reiki, angels and crystals form a soul stirring combination indeed!

There are no complicated rituals or practices you need to do to connect with the archangels. Just call on them, talk to them, write letters to them and express your gratitude for their help. Do anything that will help you connect. Once you take the first step, their energies will pour into your life and show you the path.

Archangel Ariel helps with environmental issues, animal welfare and healing, healing plants, healing the planet. The associated crystal is *rose quartz*.

Archangel Azrael helps with peaceful passing over, comfort to the grieving and heartbroken, development of counselling skills. The associated crystal is *yellow calcite*.

Archangel Chamuel helps with finding new love, friendship, career, job, lost objects, peace in relationships, healing soul mate relationships. The associated crystal is *green fluorite*.

Archangel Gabriel helps with conception, pregnancy and birth, adoption, early childhood issues, life path of spiritual teachers and writers. The associated crystal is *citrine*.

Archangel Haniel helps with menstrual cycle, hormonal issues, fertility, personal harmony, balance, honouring sensitivity. The associated crystal is *moonstone*.

Archangel Jeremiel helps with healing unhealed patterns, conducting life reviews, emotional healing. The associated crystal is *amethyst*.

Archangel Jophiel helps with clearing negative energies, artistic projects, development of inner beauty, radiating grace. The associated crystals are pink tourmaline and *rubelite*.

Archangel Metatron helps with chakra clearing, issues with older children, developing spiritual awareness in children. The associated crystal is watermelon *tourmaline*.

Archangel Michael helps with freedom from fear, safety and protection, spiritual life purpose, spiritual growth, building a healing practice, guidance or assistance for mechanical repair work, cutting energetic cords. The associated crystal is *sugilite*.

Archangel Raguel helps with conflict resolution, justice and fairness, harmony. The associated crystals are aqua aura and *aquamarine*.

Archangel Raphael helps with physical healing, good health, assistance to healers, travel safety. The associated crystals are *malachite* and *emerald*.

Archangel Raziel helps with clairvoyance, manifestation, third eye healing, esoteric learning, past life healing. The associated crystal is *clear quartz*.

Archangel Sandalphon helps with healing through music. The associated crystal is *turquoise*.

Archangel Uriel helps with uncovering divine wisdom, intellectual learning and growth. The associated crystal is *amber*.

Archangel Zadkiel helps with memory, spiritual teaching and learning, healing the heart. The associated crystal is *lapis lazuli*.

Full Moon Healing with the Archangels

The full moon is the perfect time for us to let go of things that no longer serve us. Recurring patterns that diminish the quality of our lives can be safely released in the light of the full moon.

Here are a few examples of what you may release during the period of the full moon:

- *Blocks to manifestation:* If you are working on specific goals but find blocks coming in the way, this may be the right time to release them.
- *Recurrent emotional patterns:* Anger, fear, resentment, envy, guilt and the like.
- *Unhelpful patterns:* An inability to trust in the flow of life, an inability to receive, feelings of powerlessness, feelings of not being good enough, victim mentality and the like.

If you like working with the angels, you can call on Archangel Haniel and Archangel Jeremiel to bless this healing ritual with their energies. Haniel's energy can help us connect with the moon and Jeremiel's energy can help us review our lives and release negative patterns from our consciousness. Alternately, you can call on other Masters/ Reiki Guides/ Spiritual Guides.

The Ritual

1. Wear a white coloured dress if you have one.

2. Step outside on the evening of the full moon. Your garden, roof terrace or balcony will work fine. If you cannot do this outdoors, you can also do it indoors, preferably near a window from which the full moon is visible.

3. Place a white coloured candle in the centre of your healing space. Make sure it is placed safely as you will need to walk around it. If you have a large outdoor area, you can light a fire instead of using the candle.

4. Call on Archangel Jeremiel and Archangel Haniel. Request them to be with you and to help you heal.

5. Look at the moon, draw the distance symbol in front of you and connect with its energy. Masters must also draw the Master Symbol.

6. Stretch your hands and invite the energy of the full moon into your space. Receive the energy with your hands. Pour the energy over yourself, starting from your head all the way down to your feet. Let your hands move over your aura so you feel the energy moving.

7. As you pour this energy over yourself, clearly state your intention to release an unhelpful pattern from your life. For example, if you carry blocks to manifestation, you could

say, "*I now release all those blocks that prevent me from manifesting at my highest potential.*" Do this three times (more if you feel like).

8. Thereafter, draw all the Reiki symbols in the air and begin walking around the candle in circles, taking care to maintain a safe distance. The Archangels will accompany you. As you walk in the light of the moon, hold a strong intention to heal this block or pattern. This act of walking with a crystal clear intention can facilitate powerful healing. The energy of the Archangels will further act as a catalyst in your healing. Continue to walk until you naturally feel like stopping.

9. Express your gratitude. Drink lots of water and rest for a while, before getting back to your routine.

For deep-rooted patterns, this ritual may need to be done more than once. Release as much as feels natural to you every full moon. You don't have to get everything accomplished the very first time. From a larger perspective, every small step we take towards healing makes a huge positive difference.

Enjoy healing in the moonlight!

Reiki Babies and Archangels – Part 1

A Reiki Baby is a child that is born into a home where Reiki is practised and the Reiki principles are lived. If you (or some of your clients) are on the road to parenthood or facing fertility issues, it may help you to learn about conscious conception. Reiki and the Archangels can help wannabe parents with conception, pregnancy and birth.

Conception and Archangel Gabriel

The conception of a baby is a divine phenomenon. When a baby is conceived with love and awareness, it makes the experience all the more divine. Babies are often conceived unconsciously and the news of pregnancy comes as a surprise to many expectant parents.

At the other end are couples with fertility issues. They struggle with conception. Women tend to get more stressed as they watch their biological clocks ticking away. Some also experience emotional turmoil as they stress over why their body is unable to do something that most other bodies can do.

I was working with a woman who had difficulty conceiving a baby. During the session, I called upon Archangel Gabriel, who is known for helping with fertility, conception and pregnancy. Gabriel had a powerful message for this woman.

She said,

"Be like an empty cup."

As I meditated on the message, its meaning became clear. Struggle always blocks the flow of energy. For any project to be successful, one must be like an empty cup that is ready to receive. If the cup is full and cannot be cleared of its contents, there is no way something new can be added to it.

So is it with the process of conception. This woman had loads of preconceived ideas about conception, fertility, pregnancy and parenting. In short, she had a cluttered cup. She was being asked to do away with all her ideas and to be like an empty cup that is open to receiving.

Fertility struggles can make the energy surrounding conception rather heavy. It is a good idea to be completely empty and conscious while trying to conceive a baby. This shifts the energy and sends out a loving vibration to the soul that is to be born. Conscious conception is significant not just for couples who have made a recent decision to conceive a baby. It is equally, if not more important, for those couples that have been trying to conceive for years.

If you've been diagnosed with fertility issues, the first thing you need to do is drop the word *infertility* from your vocabulary. By labelling yourself *'infertile'*, you add yet another unnecessary block to the path of conception. Seek medical assistance if you wish to but do not fall into the trap of using medical terminology that can create blocks to healing. Empty yourself of all labels and ideas. Focus only on love.

Conscious Conception and Reiki Babies

Conscious conception means that a baby is conceived out of pure love. It is not conceived because everyone around has kids or because of pressure from external sources. It is not conceived because the parents have unconscious ego needs and want another soul to accomplish things that they could not. There are loads of souls waiting to incarnate on Earth. When you choose to conceive because you wish to help a soul incarnate and live its intended purpose on Earth, it is an act of love. When you conceive a baby because you wish to share unconditional parental love with another soul, it is an act of love. And when something is done out of pure love, the Universe lends full support. Guidance is received, fertility struggles are overcome and conception is a joyous experience.

For conscious conception to happen, the focus must shift away from the parents and move towards the child. The couple welcome the soul from their hearts and then let go completely, allowing the soul to incarnate in divine timing. Meanwhile they prepare themselves and their home in an effort to welcome this soul. They heal themselves physically and maintain a healthy lifestyle that supports conception. They heal their own childhood emotional wounds, so as to ensure that their pain is not inflicted on their child. The wannabe parents also heal any problems in their own relationship and nurture it with unconditional love. A child that is born into such a home of love and light becomes a Reiki Baby!

The next chapter includes two powerful meditations with Reiki, Archangel Raphael and Archangel Gabriel that can help couples trying to conceive. And if you are a professional healer, it may be of help to you when you work with clients trying to conceive a baby.

Reiki Babies and Archangels – Part 2

You can use these meditations to guide clients that are trying to conceive and also to help yourself if need be. Do keep in mind that your experience with the meditation would be unique and will flow as per your need (or your client's need). Use this as a reference but trust your intuition and make changes, as you feel guided to.

Archangels Raphael and Gabriel can be called on for help with conception, pregnancy and birth.

Fertility Meditation with Archangel Raphael

Here is a powerful fertility meditation with Reiki and Archangel Raphael that can help heal blocks in the reproductive system and prepare it for conception. It can help those who are trying to conceive naturally as well as those receiving medical assistance. It can be done by men as well as women.

1. Light a green candle in a quiet clean space. Burn some incense and play soothing music.

2. Lie down and relax with a few deep breaths.

3. Call upon Archangel Raphael. Visualise him seated by your side.

4. Ask Raphael to place his hand over your reproductive system and send his healing emerald green light through it.

5. Visualise this light clearing away all blocks and making the system fertile ground for conception.

6. Next visualise Raphael placing a ball of Reiki infused with the symbols of your choice inside the system. This will ensure the energy keeps working until your next meditation.

7. Thank Raphael and Reiki for their help.

Conscious Conception Meditation with Reiki and Archangel Gabriel

This meditation helps couples connect with Gabriel and seek her assistance with conception. It also helps extend a loving invitation to the soul that would incarnate.

1. Light a pink candle in a quiet clean space. Burn some incense and play soothing music.

2. Take a few deep breaths and relax.

3. Call upon Archangel Gabriel.

4. Visualise her standing in front of you or sitting beside you.

5. Tell her of your desire to bring a baby into this world. Pour you heart out to her. Share your fears and worries. Request her to help you release your fears and blocks that may be standing in the way of conception.

6. Place your hand on your heart chakra, look skywards and say to the Universe, *"I now send my love to the soul that would find the perfect parents in me and my partner. Thank you Universe."*

7. Ask Gabriel to carry your message of love to the soul that would benefit most by being born into your home.

8. Next feel Gabriel placing her hands on your heart and sacral chakras and blessing them.

9. Visualise a pink mist descending into the room and enveloping you.

10. At this point, visualise Archangel Gabriel, placing a baby inside your womb (inside your partner's womb if you are a man).

11. Next request Reiki to form a cocoon of energy around you. Draw the power symbol and Master symbol (for third degree practitioners) on this cocoon and seal the energy.

12. Take a deep breath and completely let go of any need to control the outcome. Trust that conception will happen in divine timing.

13. Thank Gabriel and Reiki for their assistance.

The next chapter focuses on child adoption and the roles played by Reiki and the Archangels in the case of adopted children.

Reiki Babies and Archangels – Part 3

Conscious Adoption

Children are usually adopted by couples who do not have biological children. Adoption is often viewed as a last resort and something that is done when all methods to have a biological child fail. Once the child comes home, the force of love takes over and the new parents often forget that the child is not a biological one. That is the power of love. The adoption of a child can be a divine experience when a child is adopted consciously rather than as a last resort.

Just as in conscious conception, the focus in the case of adoption must be on the child and not on the parents. An adopted child must never be viewed as a replacement for a biological child; as someone who is brought in to fill the emptiness in the life of couples. A child is a child. Every child is precious, irrespective of whether he is biological or adopted. A client of mine who recently adopted a baby shared this inspiring quote, which sums up the beauty of adoption:

"Adoption means you grew in your mommy's heart instead of her tummy"- Author Unknown.

Conscious adoption happens when:

- The parents desire to share unconditional parental love with a soul that does not share their biology. This requires the heart chakra to be completely open.

- The parents choose to take responsibility for a soul that has no contact with its birth family and thereby help that soul fulfil its Earthly purpose. This is not done with a sense of Ego, where one feels he is great because he is caring for someone with no family. Instead, it is done with a sense of gratitude towards life for being blessed with a beautiful opportunity to love and parent.

Who Must Adopt?

Adoption is not just for couples who do not have biological children. It can even be considered by those that have biological children already. As stated earlier, adoption is not a replacement strategy. It is another beautiful way to build a family. However, one must be able to answer all these questions with a **'Yes'** before making the decision to adopt:

- Can you love a child not born to you as your own?

- If you have biological children already, can you bridge biological differences and allow only the power of love to reign in your family? Can you view all your children as one?

- If you do not have biological children, can you view this child with fresh eyes? Can you view him or her as your precious little baby and never as a replacement for the biological child you do not have?

Archangel Gabriel, Archangel Metatron and Reiki

If you feel a calling to adopt or you have clients that are looking at adoption, you can call upon Archangel Gabriel and Archangel Metatron. In most countries, the adoption of a child is a long journey that involves legalities and paperwork. It is often difficult for prospective parents to find children that can be adopted. But as always, when you hold a crystal clear intention enveloped in love, the Universe opens up magical new avenues and you will be led to the child that is perfect for you and your family.

If you wish to adopt because you do not have biological children, do make sure that you first heal any residual pain you may have. If you have clients who wish to adopt, help them heal all traces of old pain first and then support them on their journey towards adoption. Help them understand that when a child is adopted, it must be received with an open heart. You do not want old pain over the absence of a biological child to come in the way of bonding with a new child.

Conscious Adoption Meditation with Reiki, Archangel Gabriel and Archangel Metatron

You can use this mediation to guide clients who are looking at adopting a child and also use it yourself if need be:

1. Light a pink candle in a clean, quiet space.

2. Burn some incense and play soothing music.

3. Take a few deep breaths and relax.

4. Call on Archangel Gabriel and Archangel Metatron. Visualise them seated beside you.

5. Talk to them. Tell them of your desire to adopt a child. Share your fears with them and ask them to help you heal.

6. Request them to help you open your heart to the child that is best suited to you and your family.

7. Lie down and visualise the archangels placing their hands over your heart and blessing you.

8. Feel the love flowing from your heart. Request the archangels to carry your invitation of love to the soul that would benefit most by having you and your partner as parents.

9. Visualise the archangels flying away with your message of love.

10. After a while, visualise the archangels coming back to you with the baby or child that is perfect for you and your family.

11. Receive the child with gratitude and embrace him or her.

12. Visualise your entire family standing together- you, your partner and biological children (if any). Place this child among all of you and feel the joy overflowing from your heart. If you have biological children, see them embracing this child. Enjoy the bonding of the new siblings. What a beautiful moment it is!

13. If this is your first child, welcome him or her with love. Feel the joy of parental love flowing from your heart.

14. Feel the power of love overcoming biological barriers. A beautiful new family is formed.

15. Finally, request Reiki to form a cocoon of energy around this image. Draw the power symbol and Master Symbol on the cocoon and seal the energy.

16. Give thanks to Reiki and the Archangels for their assistance.

17. Proceed with practical steps towards adoption and completely let go of the outcome. Allow the Universe to bring you the perfect child at the perfect time!

Stress Relief with the Angels

All of us find ourselves in stressful situations from time to time. Some of us manage stress effectively while some of us struggle to cope. Some of us are calm in certain stressful situations while we freak out in other kinds of situations. Each person is different and what is stressful to you may not be stressful to your sibling or best friend.

We can get stressed as a result of work hassles, financial troubles, health issues, parenting problems, relationship troubles and the like. And when we are stressed, it is hard for us to even breathe properly, forget about thinking clearly!

Rather than struggle to arrive at logical solutions when we are too frazzled to think, we can allow ourselves to be supported by the all-loving angels. Angelic energy brings an instant sense of calm in all kinds of stressful situations. It can help us feel better, think better and cope better.

Here is a simple meditation you can do whenever you find yourself stressed.

1. Choose a quiet private room where you will be undisturbed for about ten minutes.

2. Light a candle. Draw the Reiki symbols that you are attuned to on the walls. If you are not attuned to symbols yet, you can place your palms on each wall for ten seconds and give Reiki to it.

3. Stand at the door to the room. Connect with the angels and invite them into the room. Say from your heart, *"My Dear Angels, please come into this space now. Thank you."*

4. Once you invite the angels, wait a couple of minutes at the door. You will be able to sense the angelic energies gushing in. Trust the impressions you receive.

5. Go in and close the door if you wish to. Sit on a comfortable chair or mat and request the angels to surround you. Wait till you sense that you are surrounded and safe.

6. Talk to them about the stress that you are going through. Get it off your chest. You can talk all you want, without any fear of being judged.

7. After you're done talking, lie down comfortably and request the angels to work on you. Do not instruct them on how to help you.

8. Allow the experience to unfold naturally. The angels may give you Reiki or flood you with healing light of varied colours. They may whisper soothing messages in your ears or stroke you gently and help you relax. They may even direct their energy to massage you, thereby helping you relax even more deeply. Be completely open to the

experience. Only then will you allow the angels to help you in a way that you most need it.

9. Once done, hand over the stressful situation to the angels. For instance, if you are stressed about your child, visualise placing your child in their loving hands and ask them to take care of him or her. If you are stressed about a relationship, visualise placing the relationship in the loving care of the angels.

10. Thereafter, request that hundreds of angels be present with you and with the other person (or situation) that you are stressed about.

11. Thank the Angels and Reiki for their kind assistance.

12. Wake up feeling stronger, calmer and more in balance.

This meditation can help you acquire a new perspective on any situation that causes you stress. It will also benefit everyone else involved in the situation. As hundreds of angels stay by your side, you will feel a deep sense of calm and empowerment. You will begin to view the situation from a higher perspective, thereby bringing peace, harmony and healing to you and to everyone else.

Healing the Scars of Verbal Abuse with Reiki and the Angels

Abuse can be of a physical, verbal, emotional or sexual nature. This chapter is specifically about verbal abuse. Verbal abuse often overlaps with emotional abuse. It is fairly common and is often dismissed as anger. However, there is a thin line of difference between plain anger and anger induced verbal abuse. It can be hard to pinpoint where anger ends and abuse begins. An abusive person is someone who has gone through intense pain and trauma and unconsciously inflicts the same on others. The person may be very nice most of the time. But when he is triggered, he turns into a venomous snake that bites you in the places that hurt most and poisons your body and mind.

Recall a memory when someone used manipulative tactics to intimidate you, accused you unjustly, insulted you, called you names, threatened you into submission or something similar. You were probably shocked by all the nonsense that was being said to you, but felt powerless because you could not get the other person to be fair in war.

Many of us have such experiences in different relationships, though it is more likely to occur in close relationships such as parent-child, husband-wife etc. At times, we may be the ones being abusive and inflicting pain on others with our words. We have to accept our own shadow as well.

Reiki and the Angels can help us whenever we find ourselves being abusive or abused.

If you find yourself being verbally abused by someone:

1. First of all, be assertive. Tell the person firmly but respectfully that you will not tolerate behaviour that is unfair and abusive. If the person is so absorbed in his own pain that he does not understand, just leave the place and take some time off.

2. If you feel hurt by all that was said to you, there is no need to pretend that you are very strong. Go into a private space and cry your heart out. And this is not just for women. Men have emotions too and it is OK for them to cry. Get the pain out. You will feel a lot better.

3. Draw or visualise a big Sei Hei Ki (and Master Symbol for 3rd Degree Practitioners) between you and the other person and request Reiki to heal the situation.

4. Talk to the Angels about your pain or write a letter to them. Ask them to soothe your pain and also help the other person see light. Learn to do Angel Card Readings. Card Readings are like a private consultation with the Angelic realm and they are extremely useful in guiding us and our

loved ones through turmoil. Follow the guidance you receive and just let go of the situation.

5. Wait and witness the healing that occurs spontaneously. Not only will the situation be healed in time, but you will also learn some lessons that will help you grow stronger.

If you are the one that has hurt someone with verbal abuse and you happen to regret it later, here's what can help you heal:

1. Know that feeling regret is a positive sign. It means your heart is soft enough to know that it did not act from love (which is the essence of who you are). But it is never too late to express love to someone you have hurt. Put your Ego aside and render a heartfelt apology to the person. Hug the person, look him/her in the eye and say how sorry you are.

2. If the person is still hurt and you live with the person, communicate directly with the person's soul when he/she is fast asleep. Express your feelings and apologise for the hurt caused. Tell the soul that all the rough words you used were the result of your own pain and had nothing to do with him/her. If you do not live with the person, you can still communicate with the soul over a distance. The soul will receive your message and healing will occur.

3. Draw or visualise a big Sei Hei Ki (and Master Symbol for 3rd Degree Practitioners) between you and the other person and request Reiki to heal the situation.

4. If you feel ashamed or guilty about what you did, consult with the Angels again. They will help you remember your true nature of love and innocence. They will soothe your worries and help you let go of all guilt and shame.

5. Have compassion for your own self. You have also gone through pain, which is why you reacted the way you did. This does not mean that you continue to be that way. It just means that you learn from your pain and take time to heal your own wounds.

It may take several attempts before a complete healing happens. Do not give up. And please take all the help you need from Reiki and the Angels. You do not have to suffer alone. With so much of love and guidance available to us, we never need feel alone or helpless. We are loved beyond measure and taken care of. All we need is a heartfelt willingness to heal.

Note: At times, it is impossible to heal other people no matter what you do because they have chosen their own lessons and they cannot heal until they choose to. In such cases, please do not waste your precious time hanging on to an abusive relationship. Please seek professional help and determine the best course of action for you and your relationship.

Reiki with your Guides and Angels

When was the last time you received Reiki from someone? As a Reiki healer, you probably spend plenty of time giving Reiki to others. Or maybe you give too much of yourself in general and drain your energies in the process. Do you also receive at times?

It's a different feeling altogether when you can stop giving for a bit and enjoy receiving from others!

To receive Reiki from another person, you don't need to visit a friend or a practitioner. It can be received in the comfort of your own home.

Guess from whom?

From your *Reiki Guides and Angels*!

I once had a powerful experience and learnt that it is OK for us to sit back, relax and receive Reiki at times. A rather hectic professional week had thrown me off balance. I then had a beautiful encounter with Archangel Raphael who guided me to just relax for a bit and receive Reiki from him and his team that included several guides and angels.

I had never imagined that such a thing could be possible and was rather stunned to be told this. But my body seemed delighted to receive this message from Raphael and forced me to do as instructed. I then lay down and began to receive the energy. I could sense the presence of Raphael and many guides and angels in the room. The energy was magical. I drifted into a state of deep relaxation and felt so very loved and pampered.

If you've been giving too much of yourself, it is a good idea to take these breaks and receive Reiki from higher beings. Reiki remains the same, irrespective of whether it is channeled by Reiki practitioners in human form or by Higher Beings. However, our Guides and Angels radiate unconditional love and peace while healing us with energy. This adds a whole new dimension to the Reiki experience and makes it truly divine. It also helps us absorb some of their qualities and helps us radiate love and peace when we get back to working with clients, friends and family.

Here's how you do it:

1. Light candles, burn some incense and play soothing music.

2. If you have pictures of Masters and Angels that you connect well with, place them in the room. Oracle cards work just as well.

3. Call on Archangel Raphael and all your other Reiki Guides and Angels. Request them to give you some Reiki.

4. Lie down, take a deep breath and allow yourself to receive.

5. Let go completely and allow them to work on you. Do not try to control the session or instruct them to follow any particular sequence. Just relax and go with the flow.

6. As they work on you, you may notice sensations of warmth and tingling or you may feel safe and loved. Enjoy feeling pampered.

7. Shift positions in between if you need to. You may need to lie on your stomach while they work on the back chakras.

8. Once you feel it's done, thank them for their kindness.

9. Get back to your routine feeling great!

This is not a substitute for daily self healing. It is best done whenever you've given too much of yourself or feel out of balance in general. It can also be done when you feel unwell or exhausted from a hard day's work. The idea is to help you relax and learn to receive. We must remember that the ultimate responsibility for our healing lies with us. Having said that, a bit of pampering every now and then doesn't hurt either. It only serves to compound our efforts at healing our lives!

Five Ways to Heal Yourself in Sleep

All of us know of varied ways in which we can heal ourselves when awake. We give ourselves Reiki. We meditate. We work with crystals and angels. We spend time in nature. We read, write and do innumerable things, all of which have powerful healing effects. But do you know that it is possible for tremendous healing to occur even when we are asleep?

Our logical mind shuts down during sleep and we are more open and receptive. Therefore, the sleep state is fertile ground for powerful healings of all kinds.

Here are some ways that you can heal yourself during sleep:

1. Reiki Cocoon

Before you fall asleep, request Reiki to form a cocoon of energy around you. Visualise yourself resting in this cocoon. Draw the symbols of your choice on it. Intend that this cocoon helps you heal anything that is unhealed in you. It could be a health concern, an emotional problem, stress, a relationship issue etc. Give thanks and drift into sleep. This practice done every night makes healing an ongoing process and adds value to your other healing practices. You will let go of many things that don't serve you and the process will feel quite effortless as it is done in the sleep state.

2. Letters to the Angels

Whenever you find yourself in troublesome situations, write a letter to the angels describing your situation. Pour your heart out. Request them to work on you while you sleep and to bring clarity to your mind and peace to your heart. Draw the Reiki symbols of your choice on the paper. Place the letter under your pillow; thank the angels and drift into sleep. You will receive clarity and wake up with a sense of peace.

3. Angel Cards

Working with angel cards is an effective way to receive step by step guidance for healing. That way we don't have to drive ourselves nuts over healing an entire problem and can instead take one small step at a time. Do card readings for yourself frequently. Then place the cards that were received near (or under) your pillow. Draw the Reiki symbols of your choice over the pillow and drift into sleep. You will process the guidance received and kick start healing right away. This practice done regularly heals a lot of issues. One day you will look back and witness the healing effects of this practice.

4. Programmed Crystals

Cleanse a rose quartz crystal. Give Reiki to it for a while. Request your Reiki Guides, Archangels and Angels to program the crystal with healing energy and information that would be of help in your situation. Place the crystal near you when you are asleep. It will be programmed through the night. The following night, again before going to bed, place the crystal on your third eye and absorb the healing that it has been programmed with. When you fall asleep doing this, you will be more receptive and heal faster.

5. Direct Archangel Healing

The Archangels are mighty beings who can help us heal in magical ways, provided we give them full permission to help us. Before you fall asleep, call on the Archangels that you feel connected to and request them to be present in your room through the night. Give them permission to work on you while you sleep. For instance, if you need help with physical healing, you can call on Archangel Raphael and request him to work on your health issue and to heal it completely. If you need help with fear and anxiety, you can call on Archangel Michael and ask him to do the same. This may need to be repeated on several nights until you receive a full healing.

Experiment with each of these techniques and also with a combination of techniques. You can use the combination that feels right to your situation. You can use the Reiki cocoon each night, even when you do not have major issues to heal. It can help clear away minor negativities picked up during the day and also accelerate spiritual progress.

Connecting with our Guardian Angels

We all have guardian angels who have been assigned the role of being in charge of our safety and welfare on Earth. It is possible for us to form a conscious connection with our guardian angels. It is said that we are normally assigned two guardian angels each. But I have observed during meditations that some people only sense the presence of one guardian angel. It does not matter whether we have one, two or even more than two. What is more important is connecting with their energies.

There are two ways of connecting with them:
1. Meditation
2. At Bedtime

Meditation

This is a very simple meditation that can be done anytime.

1. Sit or lie down comfortably. Light a candle and play some soothing music if you like.

2. Close your eyes and take a few deep breaths.

3. Draw the distance symbol in the air.

4. Open up your palms, such that they are facing up. Start the flow of Reiki and visualise the energy forming a bridge between you and your guardian angels. You can visualise your angels standing at the other end of the bridge if you wish to.

5. Say these words: *"My Dear Guardian Angels, please connect with me now. Thank you."* Your open palms serve as an invitation for your angels to connect with you.

6. Trust the impressions you receive. You may feel someone placing their palms in yours. Your palms may feel warm or tingly. Or you may just know that your guardian angels are by your side. You may sense the presence of one, two or more angels. Whatever you experience is fine.

7. Slowly draw your palms towards your chest and keep them crossed over your heart chakra. This will draw the loving energies of your guardian angels into your heart.

8. Express your gratitude to your angels, *"Please guide me and help me with my purpose here on Earth. Thank you for being my guardian angels."*

9. Open your eyes when ready and get back to your routine.

At Bedtime

This is very relaxing and highly recommended! It can be done every night and is particularly comforting if you've had a hard day.

1. Once you are in bed and ready to fall asleep, request your guardian angel to sit behind you, such that his or her lap is over your pillow.

2. Raise your head slightly and place it on the angel's lap. Physically, your head would still be on the pillow but energetically you will sense a difference. Feel the comfort and warmth emanating from your guardian angel. You may sense the angel stroking your forehead with love. It is deeply relaxing! Enjoy being cared for and pampered.

3. You will fall asleep feeling safe, peaceful and loved.

Note: If you connect with two or more guardian angels, you can request one of them to sit each day. Or do it any other way as per your intuitive guidance. There is no right and wrong.

Angel Communication through Letters

Do you feel connected to the angelic realm?

Does the subject of angels fascinate you?

Are you open to working with the angels?

If you answered yes to even one of the above questions, you can begin connecting with our dear friends in the angelic realm right away!

All you need are a pen and a sheet of paper.

One of the easiest ways to communicate with the angels is by writing letters to them. Remember the good old-fashioned days when many of us wrote letters to friends and family? That's one of the best ways to communicate with the angels even in the current age of technology! You can type out your letter if you wish to. But hand written letters are always better because they are infused with more of your personal energy.

What to write about?

You can write to the angels about anything that you wish to share or communicate. There are really no rules. You can write to them about:

- Your desire to connect with them
- How you are feeling on a given day
- How your week has been
- How your life is going
- Your relationships
- Your fears and worries
- The happy moments in your life
- The stressful moments in your life
- Any challenges you may be facing related to health, career, finances, relationships etc. and assistance you may need
- Your Reiki practice and any assistance you may need with the same
- Anything and everything! Remember the angels love us unconditionally. So, we can feel free while writing to them. We can communicate with them just like we would communicate with a good friend. No inhibitions, no analysis, no worries about grammar, language and punctuation. The only requirement is that you write from your heart. This is powerful.

Where to keep your letters

Once your letter is ready, you can place it:

- Under your pillow
- In a special box or purse
- In your deck of angel cards
- Under crystal angels

- In your Reiki box
- In your private journal
- Any other space that feels right to you

Here is an example of a general heartfelt letter to the angels.

My Dear Angels,
Thank you for being part of my life. My week has been good this far and I feel so grateful for everything in my life. I spent some quality time with my family and enjoyed every moment of it. I have been practising Reiki regularly and I intend to stay motivated to practise every day. I am so happy to have you as part of my life. Please help me connect with you more often. Please shine your light through me so I may heal myself and thereby help heal the world.
Thank you.
I love you
Your Name

Here is an example of a letter that can be written when you need specific assistance with any issue.

Dearest Angels,
I have been rather stressed this week. I have too many worries on my mind. I am anxious about how my life will unfold. I need help with being more trusting and relaxed. I hand over all my worries to you. I also give you the permission to help me heal my body, mind and spirit so I may flow with life and enjoy every moment. Please help me. Thank you so much for being part of my life.
Lots of Love
Your Name

These are just sample letters to help you get going. Tailor your letter to express your personal concerns and to communicate with the angels about the happenings in your life.

Write as many letters as you wish to. Place the letters between your palms and give them some Reiki if you wish. You can write these letters on a daily, weekly or monthly basis. Go through your stack of letters every once in a while and discard the ones whose purpose is complete.

Trust that your messages will reach the angels. Be open to any assistance or healing that comes your way. There is really no way to know beforehand about how the angels will reach out to you. So, stay completely open and allow the angelic magic to unfold!

Reiki Journal for Healing and Communication with Higher Realms

The written word is powerful. Writing is an effective way to facilitate healing. And for this, we are going to use a nice healing instrument called a Reiki Journal.

A Reiki Journal is a book in which you can record your experiences and intentions, gain clarity on troublesome issues, communicate with guides and angels and express yourself without any inhibitions. A Reiki Journal is special because it is infused with Reiki and everything that goes into in would receive Reiki. It can be a faithful friend to you and help you in amazing ways. It can help you keep track of your progress with healing as you can always go back and refer to it anytime.

Create your Reiki Journal

1. Choose a book that appeals to you.
2. Before you begin using it, give Reiki to it for a few minutes. Place your palms on the book and bless it.

3. Draw the Reiki symbols on the first page and decorate it in any other way that you feel like.

Your journal is ready for use!

Uses of a Reiki Journal

The Reiki Journal can be used in two ways. One is for self expression and the other is for communication with Guides and Angels. Remember to date each journal entry, as it will help you track your progress over time.

Self Expression

This means you just express yourself from time to time. You can write about:

- Your experiences of the day and any significant events that transpired
- Your feelings and the positive and negative emotions you felt during the day
- Any healing you experienced and any learning that happened
- The things and people you are grateful for in your life
- Anything and everything that will help you grow as a person

Remember your journal is a friend and a healing instrument. So, write without inhibitions, as that is when it will fetch best results. Draw any symbols that you are guided to alongside your writing. Give Reiki to your writing for a minute or so or just place a ball of Reiki over it to keep the energy working. This practice can help you achieve amazing clarity of mind.

Communication with Guides and Angels

You can also use your journal to communicate with beings from higher realms such as Reiki Guides, Angels, Archangels and Ascended Masters. This can be in a question answer format, where you note down your question and then record the answer that your guides and angels give you. Alternately, you can just describe your issue, surrender the issue and then allow healing to take place in its own time.

If you wish to communicate with Higher Beings and receive guidance from them through your writing, you will need to put your logical mind aside and trust your intuition.

Here's how you do it:

1. Create a meditative space by lighting a candle and playing some soothing music.

2. Take a few deep breaths and connect with your Masters, Guides and Angels. Request them to deliver guidance through your writing.

3. Visualise a shield of white light around you (including your journal and pen) and intend that nothing other than true spiritual guidance is able to penetrate your field.

4. Place a ball of Reiki over the page and then write down your question.

5. Without pausing to think, write down the next few words that come spontaneously to you. This is your guidance from the higher realms; the answer to your question. This process, which is often referred to as *channeling* can be done by everyone. It just takes some practice and a willingness to trust your intuition. The trick is to write down whatever

pops into your awareness spontaneously and to not get hung up on analysing the information. If you stop to analyse, the flow is lost and the information coming in can no longer be guaranteed to be accurate.

6. Keep in mind that true spiritual guidance would not be scary or harmful to you or anyone else. It will always feel safe, loving and empowering. If you receive guidance that does not feel right, discard it and do the exercise again after a while.

7. When you intuitively feel that you must stop, you can stop writing. Thank your Higher Self and all the Higher Beings who communicated their guidance to you. Read all that has been recorded and interpret the guidance in the context of your situation. Proceed with action steps to implement this guidance in your life.

This exercise will help awaken the wisdom that is latent in you. Your Masters, Guides and Angels are not telling you something you don't already know. They are only helping you discover the answers to all the questions that you have!

This exercise can empower you to heal independently more often. If it seems difficult, you can start by asking simple questions and move on to the more challenging ones when you are more confident. Be patient with yourself and keep practising as practice makes perfect.

Enjoy journaling!

Being a Reiki Angel on Earth

Many of us Reiki healers integrate Angel Healing with Reiki. We take the assistance of the angels all the time. We enjoy being cared for and loved unconditionally by these Higher Beings. We are empowered by the loving warmth that envelops us when the angels shine their light upon us.

Can we also make the effort to be Angels for others in the world; for our Reiki clients, for our friends and family, for plants, animals and even so called non-living things?

Here are six ways that we can be Reiki Angels on Planet Earth:

Smile

When was the last time you smiled from your heart? Smiling is contagious and puts people at ease. Smile at your clients and make them feel welcome. People are often nervous when they come in for healings and classes (much like how one feels when waiting to meet a doctor). When you smile from your heart, it breaks the ice and makes the person comfortable. We often forget to smile at our partners, children, family and friends. We may not even find it necessary because we see these people all the time. But that's the whole point isn't it? The people close to us share their love with us. They do so much for us that we may not always be conscious of. Make frequent eye contact with people at home and smile. Be an angel and make them feel loved and cared for.

Be Gentle Yet Firm

The angels are very gentle beings. They never intimidate us or force things down our throat. But when we seek their help, they are firm and expect that we follow the divine guidance they send our way. There is no way we can manipulate the angels into helping us with things that are not in our highest interest. Nor will they interfere with our free will unless we give them permission to help. We can help our clients best when we follow the same approach. Never promise to do things that you know are not in a client's best interest. Just to keep clients happy, don't offer to give Reiki to heal situations or force outcomes that don't feel right. It is not going to work anyway. It does not matter even if clients don't like you for not listening to them. View every case form a higher perspective and guide people like an angel would do.

Empower

The angels guide and help us when we call on them. At the same time, they also encourage us to connect with our innate power and wisdom. They strive to empower us. When clients seek help, it is our job to guide and support them to the extent necessary. But rather than make them dependent on us, we can empower them to connect with their own source of strength. It is not healthy to encourage relationships in which the teacher is viewed as the ultimate authority and the student becomes overly dependent on the teacher. Support your clients but draw the line where necessary. Ever heard the saying:

"You have to be cruel to be kind."

This is valid in certain cases and is a necessity with clients who seek comfort in dependent relationships. It is ultimately for their higher good.

Drop Judgement

This is tough but it must be done if we are to shine our light on the world. The angels see our true colours but they never judge us based on what they see. Instead, they radiate loving kindness, peace and compassion. In order to be an angel on Earth, try your best to drop all judgements. No matter how much someone may put you off, try to view him or her with compassion. People do the best they can with their level of awareness. So, drop judgement. Often, just being in the company of someone who does not judge can have a healing effect on others. Your clients are bound to heal faster when you create an environment of non-judgement and work with them from a place of compassion. Our job is to help people heal and not to hurt them more than they've already been hurt.

Lead by Example

The angels never blow their own trumpets to display their love and magnanimity to the world. Instead, they just radiate their love and inner beauty. This has a healing effect on everyone around them. Being human, we can never be perfect all the time. But we can strive to **become** the change that we wish to see in the world. If you want more kindness, be kind. If you want more love, radiate love. If you want more peace in the world, be peaceful yourself. Inspire others with your being rather than with talking and doing. Just this act of being the change you wish to see in the world can cause profound healing for those around you and for the planet.

Bless

Shower Reiki blessings upon everything you encounter. Bless the plants, trees, birds and other creatures in your environment. Bless the people who help you directly as well as indirectly. Bless you family, friends, children and clients. Bless things that appear to be non-living too. Whenever you have a moment and can remember to bless, just bless whatever is within your reach in that moment. The more we bless, the more love and light we create. In short, we live like angels.

Starting this moment, unfold your wings and be a Reiki Angel on Planet Earth!

Reiki and Spiritual Growth: A Personal Story

This is dedicated to everyone who might be feeling lost and stuck. A lot of people on Earth, including those on the spiritual path, are feeling this way now.

Dear Friend, your challenges are part of your soul's growth. One day you will see that you have come a long way and that the journey was worth every bit! Just don't give up on Reiki, ever! Reiki is your guiding light. Allow it to lead you on your journey towards spirit.

This is my own story of how Reiki led me from physical detoxification to emotional healing and finally put me on the road to spiritual growth. I hope from my heart that this helps you in whatever way is right for you.

I was always fascinated with Reiki and energy healing. But when I first approached my Reiki Master in 2007, it was not because I wanted to learn Reiki myself or grow spiritually. It was because I wanted to heal deep-rooted fears that had been bothering me for several years. I went with the hope that Reiki would work like a magic wand and my fears would fly out of the window, never to return again! Little did I know that taking this small step towards healing those innocent looking fears would lead me on a dramatic journey of unearthing deep rooted pain and initiate deep spiritual growth.

My Reiki Master did a few of sessions of healing on me. I began to feel better. She also encouraged me to learn Reiki, so I could heal myself independently. This is the best piece of advice I have received in life so far! Given the fact that I was always drawn to energy healing, I made the decision to learn Reiki pretty quickly. In less than a month of the first healing session, I was attuned to the first level of Reiki. I began to experience profound healing immediately. Even before the class was over, I developed physical symptoms such as cold and fever. The symptoms worsened as I made my way back home and continued to grow worse over the next two days. I was in the midst of an intense healing crisis. My teacher encouraged me to accept the crisis and not give in to fear.

My body went through a major detoxification. I was working at another job then and had to take off from work for a couple of days. Towards the end of the 21-day cleansing process, I was perfectly fine and felt wonderful. Blessings flooded my life soon after. Situations and people that were not serving my highest good began moving out of my life and it all happened pretty quickly! I also met my soul mate, whom I later went on to marry. This was the best blessing I received. Painful relationships over years had left me feeling drained and exhausted. Reiki helped me understand that I had been creating my reality all along and that I had the power to change the outcome of future relationships. This shift in belief combined with regular Reiki practice brought my soul mate into my life.

Life was on a high for a few months and everything seemed perfect. I was grateful to Reiki for creating such a dramatic turnaround in my life and filling it with amazing blessings.

Inspired by all the positive changes that happened, I signed up for Level 2 some months later. The class went well and I returned home feeling physically fine (unlike after Level 1). But during the 21 day cleansing process, I noticed that my hands felt stuck to my solar chakra every time I practised self-healing. The solar chakra took up almost as much energy as all of the other chakras put together. After some days, I experienced another healing crisis. And this time, a lot of fears and insecurities that lay buried in my subconscious surfaced. Incidentally, many of these issues were to do with the solar chakra, such as feelings of unworthiness, a need for approval, a need to prove my point etc. I became frightened, as the feelings were very intense. My Reiki teacher reassured me that this was also part of the healing, but I had difficulty accepting it because it was so very painful. I struggled with these symptoms for many weeks and also began to feel that Reiki had let me down by making things worse than they were. Eventually, I (the Ego part of me) began to doubt the power of Reiki, as the Ego always wants quick results! In time, I grew frustrated and stopped practicing Reiki.

Life went on and I continued working at an unsatisfactory job for four years. Along the way, I faced some personal and professional challenges (all related to the solar chakra), which I attempted to resolve only with my logical mind. But this approach left me stuck in loops of unhealthy patterns that stripped me of my inherent power and wisdom. In hindsight, I understood that my inability to accept the healing crisis after Level 2 had left me in this mess. When we refuse to accept something that comes up for healing, the same stuff keeps coming up until we learn the lesson it wants us to learn.

Interestingly, despite my decision to stop Reiki practice, I felt periodic urges to give myself Reiki. I gave in to the urges because I knew that I would feel wonderful after giving myself a Reiki treatment. I felt sad because I realised that a part of me really loved Reiki. However, another part of me (the Ego) rejected it as it could not handle the healing crises that it put me through.

It was in the significant year 2012, that Reiki made a grand re-entry into my life! As you might be aware, plenty of changes happened on Earth in 2012 and affected many people, including me (though I was not aware of it at that point). I felt the need to connect with the spiritual part of me again. I had stayed too long with just my ego and logical mind and life had become meaningless. My soul was crying out and I could not deny my spiritual side anymore.

I started by communicating with the angels. As I was in a lot of pain and confusion, I only felt comfortable talking to the loving angels. Help came from the angels. I was brought in contact with a few kind teachers who helped me heal in their own unique ways. As I received support from these teachers, I also made the decision to start my Reiki practice again. And this time, I decided to practise without any expectations. I suddenly developed the strength to accept everything that came up as part of my healing. And lo and behold, life changed again! A few months of Reiki practice in this mindset of "no expectation and complete acceptance" worked like magic and brought about tremendous healing in me.

I understood that healing with Reiki is much more than just making the symptoms of physical or emotional problems disappear. I understood that Reiki is more a way of life that helps you grow by peeling layer after layer of pain and subsequently healing them. The blessings of Reiki are most often noticed in hindsight. With these new insights and my experiences with healing in 2012, I felt the time had come for me to do the Master Degree.

The Master Degree brought to me its own share of blessings as well as challenges. I received all the blessings with joy. And to help me with the challenges, Reiki made me cross paths again with some wonderful Masters in different fields of alternate healing. I integrated all the wisdom I gained from those Masters with my Reiki practice and this wisdom is what I am trying to live today!

I am still learning. As I teach others, I also learn and heal myself. Deeper layers of pain come up to be healed almost every single day. The only difference is that now I don't get scared and run! Instead I reclaim my power and remind myself that I have the power to heal anything because it is all of my own creation. Reiki is my faithful companion on this journey, having led me from simple emotional healing in 2007 to a full-blown spiritual healing starting 2012. I give full credit to Reiki for guiding me to this point and for lighting every step along the way.

About the Author

Haripriya is a Reiki Master, Angel Healer, and Spiritual Teacher. She was drawn to Reiki right from her childhood and Reiki went on to become part of her life's purpose. Reiki is her constant companion from which she derives peace and contentment. After reaping the fruits of Reiki practice in her life, she was inspired to spread the joy of Reiki. She is the founder of Aananda Holistic Center where she conducts as well as teaches Reiki and Angel Healing. Haripriya resides in Bangalore, India.

Reach Haripriya at aanandaholistic@gmail.com and at Aananda Holistic Center on Facebook.

Printed in Great Britain
by Amazon